U.S. DEPARTMENT OF
ENERGY

PNNL-10855, Rev. 5

Prepared for the U.S. Department of Energy
under Contract DE-AC05-76RL01830

Assessment of Unabated Facility Emission Potentials for Evaluating Airborne Radionuclide Monitoring Requirements at Pacific Northwest National Laboratory - 2010

MY Ballinger   JM Barnett
TL Gervais

May 2011

Pacific Northwest
NATIONAL LABORATORY

Proudly Operated by **Battelle** *Since 1965*

DISCLAIMER

This report was prepared as an account of work sponsored by an agency of the United States Government. Neither the United States Government nor any agency thereof, nor Battelle Memorial Institute, nor any of their employees, makes **any warranty, express or implied, or assumes any legal liability or responsibility for the accuracy, completeness, or usefulness of any information, apparatus, product, or process disclosed, or represents that its use would not infringe privately owned rights**. Reference herein to any specific commercial product, process, or service by trade name, trademark, manufacturer, or otherwise does not necessarily constitute or imply its endorsement, recommendation, or favoring by the United States Government or any agency thereof, or Battelle Memorial Institute. The views and opinions of authors expressed herein do not necessarily state or reflect those of the United States Government or any agency thereof.

PACIFIC NORTHWEST NATIONAL LABORATORY
operated by
BATTELLE
for the
UNITED STATES DEPARTMENT OF ENERGY
under Contract DE-AC05-76RL01830

Printed in the United States of America

Available to DOE and DOE contractors from the
Office of Scientific and Technical Information,
P.O. Box 62, Oak Ridge, TN 37831-0062;
ph: (865) 576-8401
fax: (865) 576-5728
email: reports@adonis.osti.gov

Available to the public from the National Technical Information Service,
U.S. Department of Commerce, 5285 Port Royal Rd., Springfield, VA 22161
ph: (800) 553-6847
fax: (703) 605-6900
email: orders@ntis.fedworld.gov
online ordering: http://www.ntis.gov/ordering.htm

 This document was printed on recycled paper.
(9/2003)

Assessment of Unabated Facility Emission Potentials for Evaluating Airborne Radionuclide Monitoring Requirements at Pacific Northwest National Laboratory - 2010

MY Ballinger   JM Barnett
TL Gervais

May 2011

Prepared for
the U.S. Department of Energy
under Contract DE-AC05-76RL01830

Pacific Northwest National Laboratory
Richland, Washington 99352

Abstract

Assessments were performed to evaluate compliance with the airborne radionuclide emission monitoring requirements in the National Emission Standards for Hazardous Air Pollutants ([NESHAP]; U.S. Code of Federal Regulations, Title 40, Part 61, Subpart H) and Washington Administrative Code 246–247: Radiation Protection – Air Emissions. In these NESHAP assessments, potential unabated off-site doses were evaluated for emission locations at buildings that are part of the consolidated laboratory campus of the Pacific Northwest National Laboratory. This report describes the inventory-based methods and provides the results for the NESHAP assessment performed in 2010.

Summary

Assessments were performed to evaluate compliance with the airborne radionuclide emission monitoring requirements in the National Emission Standards for Hazardous Air Pollutants ([NESHAP]; U.S. Code of Federal Regulations, Title 40 Part 61, Subpart H). In these NESHAP assessments, potential unabated off-site doses were evaluated for emission locations at buildings that are part of the consolidated laboratory campus of Pacific Northwest National Laboratory (PNNL) operated by Battelle for the U.S. Department of Energy (DOE). Five of the buildings evaluated have emission units that met state and federal criteria for continuous sampling of airborne radionuclide emissions:

- 325 Building Radiochemical Processing Laboratory
- 331 Building Life Sciences Laboratory I
- 3410 Building Materials Science and Technology Laboratory
- 3420 Building Radiation Detection Laboratory
- 3430 Building Ultra Trace Analysis Laboratory

The NESHAP assessments were performed using building radionuclide inventory data obtained in 2010. The buildings that were evaluated are listed below, and those buildings with multiple emission points that were evaluated individually are footnoted. As noted, some of these buildings do not currently contain radioactive material but are in PNNL's Radioactive Material Tracking System because they have had or may have radioactive material. Other locations where PNNL tracks radioactive material but is not the sole occupant (e.g., APEL, BSEL, HAMMER, and POP) were also evaluated to determine PNNL compliance to limits, but the results of these facilities are not included in this document. In addition, the Marine Sciences Laboratory (MSL) in Sequim, WA is a Battelle-owned facility with trace quantities of radioactive material and an annual NESHAP assessment is performed for this facility. However, methods used for the MSL assessments are specific to that site and are not described in this document.

DOE-Owned Buildings

200E Prototype Surface Barrier Storage
318 Radiological Calibrations Laboratory
320 Analytical and Nuclear Research Laboratory[a]
325 Radiochemical Processing Laboratory
326 Materials Sciences Laboratory
329 Chemical Sciences Laboratory
331 Life Sciences Laboratory I
331G Integration Laboratory Building
331H Aerosol Wind Tunnel Research Facility
361 Modular Equipment Shelter (National Nuclear Security Administration)
747A Whole Body Counter

---

[a] In addition to the entire building, potential unabated emissions were calculated for other individual emission points.

3020 Environmental Molecular Sciences Laboratory
3410 Materials Science and Technology Laboratory
3420 Radiation Detection Laboratory[b]
3425 Ultra Low Background Counting Laboratory
3430 Ultra Trace Analysis Laboratory[a]

Privately Owned Buildings Located in Richland, WA

2400 Stevens Office Building
AML Atmospheric Measurements Laboratory
BSF Biological Sciences Facility
EDL Engineering Development Laboratory[c]
ESB Engineering Support Building
LSB Laboratory Support Building[b]
LSL-II Life Sciences Laboratory II
PSL Physical Sciences Laboratory[b]
RTL-520 Research Technology Laboratory
RTL-530 Research Technology Laboratory Support Building
Sigma 5 Office Building

---

[b] In addition to the entire building, potential unabated emissions were calculated for other individual emission points.
[c] Building had no radioactive material inventory at the time of the 2010 NESHAP assessment but is included here because it is listed in RMT and has had or may have radioactive material.

Acronyms and Abbreviations

AMD	aerodynamic mean diameter
ANSI	American National Standards Institute
CAP88-PC	Clean Air Act Assessment Package -1988 for Personal Computers
CFR	U.S. Code of Federal Regulations
Ci	curie
DOE	U.S. Department of Energy
DOT	U.S. Department of Transportation
EM	Effluent Management Group
EMSL	Environmental Molecular Sciences Laboratory
EPA	U.S. Environmental Protection Agency
HPS	Health Physics Society
LMF	location modification factor
MEI	maximally exposed individual
MPR	maximum public receptor
mrem	millirem
MSL	Marine Sciences Laboratory
NESHAP	National Emission Standards for Hazardous Air Pollutants
PCM	periodic confirmatory measurement
PIC	potential impact category
PNNL	Pacific Northwest National Laboratory
PSF	Physical Sciences Facility
PSL	Physical Sciences Laboratory
PTE	potential-to-emit
RMT	Radioactive Material Tracking System
RTL	Research Technology Laboratory
WAC	Washington Administrative Code
yr	year

Contents

Tables

1.0   Introduction

Requirements for sampling airborne radionuclide emissions are contained in the following regulations and guidelines:

- U.S. Code of Federal Regulations (CFR), Title 40, Subpart H: National Emission Standards for Emissions of Radionuclides Other than Radon from Department of Energy Facilities (2002) (40 CFR 61)
- Washington Administrative Code (WAC) 246-247: "Radiation Protection - Air Emissions" (WAC 2005)
- U.S. Department of Energy (DOE), DOE/EH-0173T, Environmental Regulatory Guide for Radiological Effluent Monitoring and Environmental Surveillance (DOE 1991).

These documents require the performance of continuous sampling at emission points that have a potential-to-emit (PTE)[d] ≥ 0.1 millirem per year (mrem/yr) off-site maximum public receptor (MPR) dose if routine emissions were not mitigated by engineered pollution control systems.

In response to these requirements, the potential unmitigated off-site receptor dose from the buildings at Pacific Northwest National Laboratory (PNNL)[e] that contain radioactive materials or sources is evaluated annually. These evaluations were performed initially in 1991 for the PNNL facilities on the Hanford Site. Based on the initial assessments, four PNNL buildings were identified as containing a sufficient inventory of radioactive material that unmitigated emissions could potentially result in an annual off-site maximum receptor dose of ≥ 0.1 mrem. These buildings are the 324 Waste Technology Engineering Laboratory, the 325 Radiochemical Processing Laboratory, the 327 Postirradiation Testing Laboratory, and the 3720 Environmental Sciences Laboratory. In accordance with the NESHAP, qualifying emission points from these buildings were sampled continuously.

The original radionuclide assessments were updated annually. The number and status of buildings evaluated has changed as buildings were transitioned to other contractors, new buildings were added, or laboratory missions were changed. The NESHAP assessments include all PNNL buildings with radioactive materials. This document describes the methodology used and reports summary results for those PNNL buildings. Results of the 1992–1993 assessment were documented by Sula and Jette (1994), with updates to this document in 1995, 1999, 2001, 2003, and 2008 (respectively Ballinger, Jette, and Sula 1995; Ballinger et al. 1999, 2001, 2003; Ballinger, Barfuss, and Gervais 2008). This report describes the current methodology for preparing the annual NESHAP assessment for 2010.

---

[d] PTE is defined as the rate of release of radionuclides from an emission unit based on the actual or potential discharge of the effluent stream that would result if all abatement control equipment did not exist, but operations are otherwise normal.

[e] PNNL is operated by Battelle for DOE under Contract DE-AC05-76RL01830.

2.0 Assessment Methodology

This section describes the methods used by PNNL to determine the potential emissions of radioactive materials from buildings operated by Battelle.

2.1 Projections of Annual Emission Quantities

Several methods for projecting potential unmitigated annual emission quantities are prescribed in WAC 246-247:

- apply an annual release fraction to the radionuclide inventory in the building
- multiply actual measured annual emissions by control system decontamination factors
- add actual measured annual emission quantities to actual measured quantities retained by control systems
- measure the annual discharge upstream from all control devices.

The inventory-based assessment method[f] has been used by PNNL since the initial building assessment in 1991. The inventory method yields an assessment based on the current building status (or even the future status if projected future inventory quantities are used in the assessment), while the other prescribed methods yield an assessment based on past building measurements. The inventory method may be more appropriate for use at research and development facilities where types and quantities of radionuclides may change and where historical sampling data may not be a reliable predictor of future emissions.

Since 2006, PNNL has maintained radioactive inventory information using the Radioactive Material Tracking (RMT) System,[g] a web-based software tool that supports real-time tracking of radioactive materials. The RMT System provides a process to comply with numerous regulatory requirements pertaining to radioactive material management. Appendix A provides a summary of the database features that apply to radioactive air emissions. The RMT System is updated by radioactive material custodians as well as other users with unescorted access to radioactive material. The software allows the approved user to add, move, modify, and ship radioactive materials in and out of PNNL buildings and verifies that building radioactive material inventory limits have not been exceeded with any inventory update. The RMT also has extensive search and report capabilities. For buildings with multiple emission points, RMT has the capability to verify compliance within building zones. This capability has not yet been employed for some

---

[f] This method is described in WAC 246-247-030 as follows: Multiply the annual possession quantity of each radionuclide by the release fraction for that radionuclide, depending on its physical state. Use the following release fractions: 1) 1 for gases, 2) 10^{-3} for liquids or particulate solids, and 3) 10^{-6} for solids. Determine the physical state for each radionuclide by considering its chemical form and the highest temperature to which it is subjected. Use a release fraction of 1 if the radionuclide is subjected to temperatures at or above its boiling point; use a release fraction of 10^{-3} if the radionuclide is subjected to temperatures at or above its melting point, but below its boiling point. If the chemical form is not known, use a release fraction of 1 for any radionuclide that is heated to a temperature of 100°C or more, boils at a temperature of 100°C or less, or is intentionally dispersed into the environment.

[g] RMT is not used by the Marine Sciences Laboratory (MSL) in Sequim, WA because MSL has a small number of radionuclides with unit doses unique to that site. An annual inventory-based assessment is performed at MSL similar to that described here but with site-specific calculations.

spaces ascertained to have unfiltered emission units in FY 2010 (e.g., 320 and 3430 perchloric acid hoods). In these cases, calculations were performed in spreadsheets using data downloaded from RMT and from other sources to estimate emissions, and signature reports were manually generated outside of RMT.

The PNNL Effluent Management (EM) Group annually requests that RMT custodians review and verify current radioactive inventory as well as throughput and proposed radioactive additions in the upcoming year. This request is made for each of the PNNL divisions through a central point of contact, who then requests inventory information from custodians in his/her organization.

The radioactive material custodians verify the RMT inventory for material under their scope of responsibility. For the 2010 assessment, effort was made to include potentially contaminated liquid research samples or wastewater that had been released from radiological control due to their low concentrations of radioactivity. The custodians enter and manage inventory representing current materials in the building, and the RMT Administrator enters and maintains data representing additional radioactive materials that may be processed in the coming year including throughput for normal operations,[h] anticipated new work, and emission of gases. Data from the Radioactive Air Gas Inventory Database are used as a resource to populate expected gas emissions for the coming year. The RMT Administrator assigns a radioactive material custodian as appropriate for the additional information, and the custodian reviews and verifies the complete set of data under his/her name. The RMT generates NESHAP reports for each building that list RMT inventory items, summarizes the total PTE, and identifies the percent of each isotope in the inventory contributing to the PTE. As mentioned previously, some NESHAP reports were generated outside of RMT in 2010 for individual emission units that compose a sub-component of total building emissions. Also, several new buildings known collectively as the Physical Sciences Facility (PSF) were completed in 2010, and radioactive material was being moved into these buildings (i.e., 3410, 3420, 3425, and 3430) at the time of the 2010 Assessment. Because these buildings were in transition, RMT data were downloaded and supplemented with additional information on inventory to be transferred or added to the building in the coming year.

Radionuclides meeting either of the following criteria are excluded from the assessments:

- radionuclides present in commercially available building/construction materials
- radionuclides that can be purchased or possessed without a special radioactive materials license.

The data are reviewed and revised as needed to eliminate duplicate information and to obtain additional information as necessary. The review process is then documented and filed with the EM File Plan.

Potential release fractions for radionuclides are based on the physical form of the radionuclide as shown in Table 2.1. Radionuclides present as sealed sources or in sealed,

---

[h] A recent update to RMT calculates throughput for the previous year and provides a field for custodians to record items on order and any expected changes in throughput for the future year. This update went into effect just after the 2010 NESHAP assessment.

unvented U.S. Department of Transportation (DOT) shipping containers are assumed to be unavailable for release under normal circumstances.

Table 2.1. Physical Forms and Potential Annual Release Fractions for Radionuclides

Form	Description	Potential Release Fraction*
Gas	Radioactive material in a gaseous or vapor form.	1
Gas (unopened cylinder)	Radioactive material in gaseous form in unopened commercial gas cylinders.	10^{-3}
Liquid (heated > boiling point)	Radioactive liquid heated to a temperature greater than its boiling point any time during the calendar year.	1
Liquid	Radioactive material is a liquid, solution, or slurry and its primary container will be opened at some point during the calendar year.	10^{-3}
Liquid (unopened container)	Radioactive liquid in an air-tight container that is not opened, or planned to be opened through the calendar year.	10^{-6}
Powder	Radioactive material will be present in powder form (i.e., particulate solid.	10^{-3}
Powder (unopened container)	Radioactive powder in an air-tight container that is not opened or planned to be opened through the calendar year.	10^{-6}
Solid (heated > melting point)	Radioactive solid heated to a temperature greater than its melting point anytime during the calendar year.	10^{-3}
Solid	Radioactive material is a monolithic solid or consists of relatively large chunks.	10^{-6}
Solid (unopened container)	Radioactive solid in a leak-proof, rigid container that is not opened or plan to be opened through the calendar year.	0
Sealed source: any type	Radioactive source manufactured, obtained, or retained for the purpose of utilizing the emitted radiation. The sealed radioactive source consists of a known or estimated quantity of radioactive material contained within a sealed capsule, sealed between layer(s) of non-radioactive material, or firmly fixed to a non-radioactive surface by electroplating or other means intended to prevent leakage or escape of the radioactive material.	0

*Based on Table 1 of the American National Standards Institute (ANSI)/Health Physics Society (HPS) N13.1-1999 (ANSI/HPS 1999).

2.2 Unit Dose Calculation

For unit dose calculations, the off-site maximally exposed individual (MEI) is defined as an individual whose residence location, work location, and lifestyle maximize the potential dose from airborne pathways. All potential environmental transport pathways associated with an airborne radionuclide release were included (i.e., air inhalation, air submersion, exposure to deposited radionuclides, and ingestion). This is a prospective dose based on estimated potential emissions from new or modified emission units and is used in determining emission monitoring requirements as part of the permitting process.

Unit dose factors for the MEI were calculated for specific radionuclides using the U.S. Environmental Protection Agency (EPA) compliance code (Clean Air Act Assessment Package – 1988 for Personal Computers [CAP88-PC]; Chaki and Parks 2000; Rosnick 2007). Radionuclides that were not represented in CAP88-PC were conservatively assigned default values, usually equal to that of [241]Am for alpha emitters or ^{137}Cs for non-alpha emitters or as indicated in the unit dose documents. The decay of the daughter products was also considered in assigning default values for short half-life radionuclides. The unit dose release factors were calculated for the Hanford Site and for the PNNL Site (Diediker et al. 2006;[i] Rhoads and Barnett 2009). These documents describe the methods and assumptions used and provide unit dose factors for the 300 Area and for the PNNL Site.

For the PSF, which includes buildings 3410–3440, and the Environmental Molecular Sciences Laboratory (EMSL), dose assessments were performed using unit doses for the PNNL Site. For buildings not on the Hanford or PNNL Sites (i.e., located in Richland), dose assessment were performed by applying a location modification factor (LMF) to the 300 Area unit dose factor to correct for varying source-receptor distances and directions. The LMF was calculated by dividing the atmospheric dispersion values (Chi/Q) for this building by the atmospheric dispersion values for the 300 Area.[j] The compliance code CAP88-PC was used to calculate these dispersion values.

2.3 Potential Emission Dose Assessment

Doses from projected radionuclide emissions were calculated by multiplying the quantity of each radionuclide present in the building by its associated potential release fraction, the 300 Area or PSF unit dose release factor and, if necessary, the LMF. Doses from individual radionuclides were summed to derive the total potential unabated annual emission dose for each building.

The facility radionuclide NESHAP assessments were prepared for each building and contained the raw inventory information, any communications clarifying or correcting the inventory information, summarized inventory information, and a cover sheet showing the resulting dose and approval signatures. The assessments were independently reviewed and subsequently approved by the preparer, technical reviewer, divisional points of contact for the inventory custodians, and the applicable building manager. After approval, assessments are maintained as records in the EM Group File Plan.

---

[i] Unit doses for the Hanford Site are in the process of being updated. DOE/RL-2006-29, Revision 1 was issued in August 2010 with unit doses calculated using CAP88-PC Version 3 (Rhoads et al. 2010). Implementation of the new unit doses in RMT is planned for January 2011.

[j] As part of the RMT update to new unit doses for the 300 Area, the LMFs for the Richland facilities will also be updated and will be changed to LMFs based on Chi/Q ratios to the PNNL Site unit doses.

3.0 Reports

Three reports are generated from RMT for the NESHAP assessment for inclusion in the final packet:

- A report of individual items provided by the RMT System, including current inventory and additional inventory expected to be processed in the coming year or brought in as part of new work. This includes potential gas emissions.
- A summary page listing the potential dose (mrem/yr) for the building inventory with sign-off blocks.
- A complete listing of each radioisotope present in the building, associated dose contribution (mrem), and the percent of the total dose for the building.

A summary of the assessment results for 2010 is provided in Table 3.1.

Table 3.1. Emission System Potential Dose Assessment Summary

Emission System	Emission Type*	System Description	Emission Measurement Required	Potential Off-site Dose mrem/yr	Comment
Systems Located on the Hanford Site					
318	Point	Radiological Calibrations Laboratory	Periodic	4.22E-06	Primarily sealed and check sources
320	Point	Analytical and Nuclear Research Laboratory	Periodic	6.72E-03	
320-115P-S	Point	Analytical and Nuclear Research Laboratory – Perchloric Hood	None	9.00E-17	trace quantities
320-133P-S	Point	Analytical and Nuclear Research Laboratory – Perchloric Hood	None	9.00E-17	trace quantities
320-138P-S	Point	Analytical and Nuclear Research Laboratory – Perchloric Hood	None	9.00E-17	trace quantities
320-144P-S	Point	Analytical and Nuclear Research Laboratory – Perchloric Hood	None	9.00E-17	trace quantities
320-165-V	Point	Analytical and Nuclear Research Laboratory – Lab Vent	None	0	
320-185-V	Point	Analytical and Nuclear Research Laboratory – Lab Vent	None	4.59E-07	trace quantities
325	Point	Radiochemical Processing Laboratory	Continuous	1.01E+02	
326	Point	Materials Sciences Laboratory	Periodic	1.37E-03	
329	Point	Chemical Sciences Laboratory	Periodic	1.37E-02	
331	Point	Life Sciences Laboratory I	Continuous	1.53E-01	
331G	Point	Integration Laboratory Building	None	0	sealed sources
331H	Point	Aerosol Wind Tunnel Research Facility	None	0	sealed sources
361	Fugitive	Modular Equipment Shelter	None	2.26E-07	
200E Storage	Fugitive	Prototype Surface Barrier Storage	None	0	sealed sources
Systems Located on the PNNL Site					
3020 (EMSL)	Point	Environmental Molecular Sciences Laboratory	None	0	sealed sources

Emission System	Emission Type*	System Description	Emission Measurement Required	Potential Off-site Dose mrem/yr	Comment
3410 (PSF)	Point	Materials Science and Technology Laboratory	Continuous	3.91E-06	
3420 (PSF): Filtered	Point	Radiation Detection Building	Continuous	9.22E-03	
3420 (PSF): Unfiltered	Point	Radiation Detection Building	None	3.5E-08	
3425 (PSF)	Fugitive	Ultra Low Background Counting Laboratory	None	3.94E-10	
3430 (PSF): Filtered	Point	Ultra Trace Analysis Building	Continuous	1.62E-03	
3430 (PSF): Unfiltered	Point	Ultra Trace Analysis Building	None	1.43E-07	
3430-1606P-S	Point	Ultra Trace Analysis Building – Perchloric Hood	None	1.06E-12	trace quantities
3430-1608P-S	Point	Ultra Trace Analysis Building – Perchloric Hood	None	1.06E-12	trace quantities
3430-1610P-S	Point	Ultra Trace Analysis Building – Perchloric Hood	None	1.06E-12	trace quantities
3430-1612P-S	Point	Ultra Trace Analysis Building – Perchloric Hood	None	1.06E-12	trace quantities
3430-1614P-S	Point	Ultra Trace Analysis Building – Perchloric Hood	None	1.06E-12	trace quantities
Systems Located in Richland					
747A	Fugitive	Whole Body Counter	None	0	sealed sources
2400 Stevens	Fugitive	2400 Stevens Office Building	None	0	sealed sources
AML	Fugitive	Atmospheric Measurements Laboratory	None	0	sealed sources
BSF	Fugitive	Biological Sciences Facility	None	0	sealed sources
EDL	Fugitive	Engineering Development Laboratory	None	0	Sealed sources; no radioactive inventory at time of 2010 assessment
ESB	Fugitive	Engineering Support Building	None	0	sealed sources
LSB	Fugitive	Laboratory Support Building	None	0	Sealed sources; no radioactive inventory at time of 2010 assessment
LSL-II	Point	Life Sciences Laboratory II	None	6.76E-10	inventory based
PSL	Point	Physical Sciences Laboratory	None	0	Sealed sources; no radioactive inventory at time of 2010 assessment
RTL-520	Point	Research Technology Laboratory	Periodic	4.19E-03	
RTL-530	Fugitive	Research Technology Laboratory Support Building	None	0	
Sigma-5	Point	Sigma 5 Office Building	None	0	Sealed sources

* "Fugitive emissions" are radioactive air emissions that do not and could not reasonably pass through a stack, vent, or other functionally equivalent structure and which are not feasible to directly measure and quantify. "Point source" is a discrete, well-defined location from which radioactive air emissions originate, such as a stack, vent, or other functionally equivalent structure (WAC 2005).

4.0 References

American National Standards Institute/Health Physics Society—ANSI/HPS. 1999. *Sampling and Monitoring Releases of Airborne Radioactive Substances from the Stacks and Ducts of Nuclear Facilities*. ANSI/HPS N13.1–1999, McLean, VA.

Ballinger MY, SJ Jette, and MJ Sula. 1995. *Assessment of Unabated Facility Emission Potentials for Evaluating Airborne Radionuclide Monitoring Requirements at Pacific Northwest National Laboratory - 1995*. PNL-10855, Pacific Northwest Laboratory, Richland, WA.

Ballinger MY, KD Shields, MJ Sula, and DL Edwards. 1999. *Assessment of Unabated Facility Emission Potentials for Evaluating Airborne Radionuclide Monitoring Requirements at Pacific Northwest National Laboratory - 1999*. PNNL-10855, Rev. 1, Pacific Northwest Laboratory, Richland, WA.

Ballinger MY, KD Shields, MJ Sula, DL Edwards, and TL Gervais. 2001. *Assessment of Unabated Facility Emission Potentials for Evaluating Airborne Radionuclide Monitoring Requirements at Pacific Northwest National Laboratory - 2001*. PNNL-10855, Rev. 2, Pacific Northwest Laboratory, Richland, WA.

Ballinger MY, MJ Sula, TL Gervais, and DL Edwards. 2003. *Assessment of Unabated Facility Emission Potentials for Evaluating Airborne Radionuclide Monitoring Requirements at Pacific Northwest National Laboratory - 2003*. PNNL-10855, Rev. 3, Pacific Northwest Laboratory, Richland, WA.

Ballinger MY, BC Barfuss, and TL Gervais. 2008. *Assessment of Unabated Facility Emission Potentials for Evaluating Airborne Radionuclide Monitoring Requirements at Pacific Northwest National Laboratory - 2007*. PNNL-10855, Rev. 4, Pacific Northwest Laboratory, Richland, WA.

Barfuss BC, JM Barnett, and MY Ballinger. 2009. *Pacific Northwest National Laboratory Facility Radionuclide Emission Points and Sampling Systems*. PNNL-15992, Revision 1, Pacific Northwest National Laboratory, Richland, WA.

Chaki S and B Parks. 2000. *UPDATED User's Guide for CAP88-PC Version 2.0*. 402-R-00-004, U.S. Environmental Protection Agency, Office of Radiation and Indoor Air, Washington, D.C.

Diediker LP, DJ Rokkan, K Rhoads, and LH Staven. 2006. *Calculating Potential-to-Emit Releases and Doses*. DOE/RL-2006-29, Revision 0, U.S. Department of Energy, Richland, WA.

Rhoads K and JM Barnett. 2009. *Pacific Northwest National Laboratory Site Dose-per-Unit-Release Factors for Use in Calculating Radionuclide Air Emissions Potential-to-Emit Radiological Releases and Doses*. PNNL-17847, Revision 1, Pacific Northwest National Laboratory, Richland, WA.

Rhoads K, SF Snyder, RL Aaberg, and DJ Rokkan. 2010. *Calculating Potential-to-Emit Radiological Releases and Doses*. DOE/RL-2006-29, Revision 1, U.S. Department of Energy, Richland, WA.

Rosnick R. 2007. *CAP88-PC Version 3.0 User Guide*. Office of Radiation and Indoor Air, U.S. Environmental Protection Agency, Washington, D.C.

Sula MJ and SJ Jette. 1994. *Pacific Northwest Laboratory Facilities Radionuclide Inventory Assessment CY 1992-1993*. PNL-10061. Pacific Northwest Laboratory, Richland, WA.

U.S. Code of Federal Regulations—CFR. 2002. 40 CFR 61, Subpart H. "National Emission Standards for Emissions of Radionuclides Other Than Radon From Department of Energy Facilities." U.S. Environmental Protection Agency.

U.S. Department of Energy—DOE. 1991. "Environmental Regulatory Guide for Radiological Effluent Monitoring and Environmental Surveillance." DOE/EH-0173T.

U.S. Department of Energy/Richland Operations—DOE/RL. 2010. *Radionuclide Air Emissions Report for the Hanford Site, Calendar Year 2009, Rev. 0*. DOE/RL-2010-17. Richland, WA.

U.S. Environmental Protection Agency—EPA. Clean Air Act Assessment Package – 1988 for Personal Computers (CAP88-PC). EPA compliance code.

Washington Administrative Code—WAC. 2005. "Radiation Protection - Air Emissions." WAC 246-247, Olympia, WA.

Appendix A

Radioactive Material Tracking Database Features

Appendix A
Radioactive Material Tracking Database Features

The RMT System was developed and maintained to be a web-based, real-time-management software system. RMT users update or propose radioactive materials in the system to maintain inventory management and to verify that emissions are below regulatory permitted quantities. The calculated PTE information obtained from the RMT System provides the basis to verify that each building is operating within set threshold limits. The annual NESHAP assessment process includes verification of this information and compiling it into a final report. The inventory information obtained and reported is described in Section 2.1.

Database Population

New or updated inventory information is obtained from individual research personnel who act as custodians or users of the material. The HDI Subject Area *Radioactive Material Identification, Acquisition, Storage, and Control (RCP-4.1.01)*, Section 10, Tracking Radioactive Material Inventory Using the RMT System, contains requirements for entering and maintaining inventory data. The RMT users have been granted access to the RMT System and are trained by an RMT administrator. Training is documented and maintained through the PNNL Laboratory Training Database.

The information entered into the RMT System that is pertinent to radiological air emissions includes:

- name of the staff member acting as custodian of the material
- material form—gas, liquid, powder, solid, sealed source
- nuclides[k]
- inventory in activity or concentration for each nuclide
- building and room in which material is stored or used
- specific item description and any additional comments related to the material (e.g., reference numbers on the material, whether the material is considered throughput, and a description of the material)
- RMT ID number is assigned by the database for each entry.

Additional information may be entered to assist staff in identification or management of the material.

RMT Reference Table Information

Potential dose calculations are made possible through reference table data that are run in a software stored procedure. These software stored procedures and reference tables are developed

---

[k] Appendix B provides support data for nuclides in uranium and plutonium enrichments.

and maintained as safety software under the *RMT System Quality Assurance Plan* (PNNL-FS-RMT-017). Any changes to these reference tables or processes require rigorous testing, peer review, and documentation before implementation.

Dose-per-Unit Release Factors Table—Factors for the mrem dose per curie (mrem/Ci) for different isotopes are listed in DOE/RL-2006-29, Revision 0[l] and PNNL-17847, Revision 1 for facilities on the Hanford Site and PNNL Site, respectively, and are entered as a separate table in the database.

Release Fraction Table—The release fractions for material forms (such as solids, liquids, or powders).

Location Modification Factors Table—LMF for the building from which the potential emission occurs. Unit dose factors are calculated for the worst-case off-site unit dose factor in the 300 Area (off-site MPR < 40 m release height, east). LMFs modify these doses for facilities in Richland based on a ratio of dispersion factors.[m]

Calculations

The database uses queries and macros that are applied to the inventory data to calculate the potential dose for the different PNNL buildings.

Normalizing Inventory Data—The database is designed to convert the reported mass and activity inventory units (such as g, mCi, μCi, mg, μg) to Ci units for use in subsequent calculations.

Potential Dose Calculations—Potential dose calculations are determined on a building-specific basis. The reported inventory is first converted to Ci and then is multiplied by release fraction (for form), the dose-per-unit release factor (mrem/Ci) for the specific nuclide, and the LMF.

Example: Calculate the PTE to the off-site MPR for 20 g of ^{238}U powder in the 325 Building

$$20 \text{ g} \times 3.36\text{E-7 Ci/g } ^{238}\text{U} \times 1\text{E-03} \times 66 \text{ mrem/Ci/yr} \times 1.0 = 4.4\text{E-07 mrem/yr}$$

where

20 g	=	quantity of material
3.36E-7 Ci/g	=	specific activity of ^{238}U
1E-03	=	release fraction for powders or liquids
66 mrem/Ci/yr	=	dose-per-unit release factor of ^{238}U for the off-site receptor in the east sector of the 300 Area with a < 40 m release height
1.0	=	LMF (with relation to 300 Area).

The cumulative PTE for the building is determined by summing the potential doses of each inventory entry.

---

[l] Upgrade to DOE/RL-2006-29, Revision 1 is planned for January 2011.
[m] Upgrades to the LMFs are planned for January 2011.

Reports

Three reports are generated using the database for the NESHAP assessment for inclusion in the final packet:

- a report of the itemized inventory data provided by the RMT System, including current inventory plus additional inventory anticipated to be processed in the coming year or brought in for new projects.
- a summary page listing the potential dose (mrem/yr) for the building inventory with sign-off blocks for the preparer, technical reviewer, divisional points of contact for the inventory custodians, and the applicable building manager.
- a complete listing of each radioisotope present in the building, associated dose contribution (mrem), and the percent of the total dose for the building.

Appendix B

Common Radionuclide Mixtures

Appendix B
Common Radionuclide Mixtures

For uranium and plutonium inventory items where enrichment is known but data on specific isotopic breakdown are not available, a method was devised to conservatively estimate isotopic composition. Uranium and plutonium blends can be grouped under the categories shown in Table B.1. Each of these categories represents an isotopic blend of uranium or plutonium that may be commonly found on the Hanford Site. The percentages shown are weight percent, and other components that make up the blend are other isotopes of uranium or plutonium. For aged plutonium blends, Am-241 also makes up a significant fraction.

Table B.1. Uranium and Plutonium Blend Information

Material in Inventory	Blend Information	Bin
Depleted Uranium or Uranium ≤ 0.25% U-235	Depleted Uranium	U(dep)
Natural Uranium or Uranium ≤ 0.72% U-235	Natural Uranium	U(nat)
Uranium ≤ 0.83% U-235 (commonly found at Hanford)	Hanford Uranium	U(Hanf)
Uranium Enriched ≤ 20% U-235	Uranium Enriched < 20%	U(20%)
Uranium Enriched ≤ 90% U-235	Uranium Enriched < 90%	U(90%)
Uranium ≥ 90% U-235	U-235	U-235
Plutonium with ≤ 6% Pu-240	Pu Blend with 6% Pu-240	Pu (6%)
Plutonium with ≤ 12% Pu-240	Pu Blend with 12% Pu-240	Pu (12%)
Plutonium with ≥ 12% Pu-240	Pu Blend with 24% Pu-240	Pu (24%)

Data and calculations for each of the blends are described here. Uranium blend information was obtained from Sula, Carbaugh, and Bihl (1991) and is shown in Table B.2.

Table B.2. Uranium Blend Specific Activities

Uranium Blend	Specific Activity Ci/g
U(dep)	3.64E-7
U(nat)	6.87E-7
U(Hanf)	9.0E-7
U(20%)	9.36E-6
U(90%)	6.21E-5

The data for depleted uranium, natural uranium, and uranium commonly found at Hanford are from Tables 8.2 and 8.3 of the referenced report. For the 20% and 90% U-235 blends, an equation was used to calculate specific activity. The equation was obtained from Figure 8.1 of Sula, Carbaugh, and Bihl (1991) and is back-referenced to WASH-1251 (Alexander 1974).

$$SA = (0.4 + 0.38E + 0.0034E^2) \times 10^{-6}$$

where SA = specific activity, Ci/g and
E = weight percent of U-235.

For E = 20 wt% U-235, S = 9.36E-6 Ci/g
For E = 90 wt% U-235, S = 6.21E-5 Ci/g

The uranium isotopes that contribute significantly to the activity are alpha emitters and have approximately the same dose potential per curie. Therefore, the specific activity is used in converting a known mass of uranium blend to activity, and the activity is all attributed to U-235.

The radionuclide and isotopic composition of 6% and 12% plutonium blends was also obtained from Sula, Carbaugh, and Bihl (1991). Data for these Pu mixtures prior to any decay of Pu-241 to Am-241 are shown in Table B.3 and were obtained from Tables 9.1 and 9.2 of the referenced report.

Table B.3. Isotopic Composition and Specific Activity of Pu Blends

Isotope	Specific Activity Ci/g	6% Pu mix			12% Pu mix		
		No decay wt%	40-yr decay wt%	Spec Act mix Ci alpha/g	No decay wt%	40-yr decay wt%	Spec Act mix Ci alpha/g
Pu-238	17.1	0.05	0.05	8.6E-03	0.1	0.1	1.7E-02
Pu-239	0.0621	93.0	93.0	5.8E-02	84.4	84.4	5.2E-02
Pu-240	0.227	6.1	6.1	1.4E-02	12.4	12.4	2.8E-02
Pu-241	103	0.8	0.1	*	3.0	0.45	*
Pu-242	3.92E-03	0.05	0.05	2.0E-06	0.1	0.1	3.9E-06
Am-241	3.43	0.0	0.7	2.3E-02	0.0	2.55	8.7E-02
			Total mix	1.0E-01			1.9E-01

* Pu-241 is excluded from the total mix calculation because it is a beta-emitter and the dose is insignificant compared to the dose from the other alpha-emitting radioactive materials.

Plutonium inventory items at Hanford have most likely aged for many years and contain significant amounts of Am-241.[n] A 40-year age is assumed for plutonium blend calculations and the amount of Pu-241 decayed to Am-241 is calculated using the following equation (Shleien, Slaback, and Birky 1998, pp. 3–17):

$$N/N_0 = e^{(-0.693\,t/T)}$$

where N/N_0 = the fraction of parent material left,
             t = time, and
             T = ½ life of the parent material.

Pu-241 has a half-life of 14.4 years (*Handbook of Health Physics and Radiological Health*, Third Edition, Table 8.13) and is decayed to about 15% of its original mass after 40 years, according to the above equation. Am-241 has a much longer half-life, so all of the Pu-241 that is converted to Am-241 is present. Table B.3 shows the resulting weight percent of each isotope after a 40-year decay for each of the Pu blends.

All of the isotopes in Table B.3 are alpha emitters except for Pu-241 which decays by beta emission and is much less damaging per curie than the others. The dose effect from the Pu-241 contribution is negligible compared to the rest. Thus, Pu-241 is excluded from further calculations, and the specific activity for the mix is calculated in terms of curies of alpha emitter

---

[n] Fuel reprocessing at Hanford took place from the mid 1940s to the mid 1980s (Ballinger and Hall 1991).

per gram. The specific activity of the mix is determined by summing the contributions from the alpha-emitting nuclides.

The isotopic composition for a 24% Pu blend was obtained from ANSI N317–1980, *Performance Criteria for Instrumentation Used for Inplant Plutonium Monitoring*. This document provides isotopic compositions of plutonium for different reactor types and burnup. The composition that results in the most conservative unit dose is shown in Table B.4 and corresponds to the data for boiling water reactor with 28000 MWD/T burnup with 40 years decay for Pu-241. The data in Table B.4 were taken directly from ANSI N317 and do not quite add up to 100%, most likely because of the number of significant digits used in the data.

Table B.4. Isotopic Composition and Specific Activity of 24% Pu Blend

Isotope	Specific Activity Ci/g	24% Pu mix No decay wt%	40-yr decay wt%	Spec Act mix Ci alpha/g
Pu-238	17.1	1.80	1.8	3.1E-01
Pu-239	0.0621	54.20	54.2	3.4E-02
Pu-240	0.227	23.80	23.8	5.4E-02
Pu-241	103	13.50	2.0	*
Pu-242	3.92E-03	6.40	6.4	2.5E-04
Am-241	3.43	0.00	11.5	3.9E-01
			Total mix	7.9E-01

* Pu-241 is excluded from the total mix calculation because it is a beta-emitter and the dose is insignificant compared to the dose from the other alpha-emitting radioactive materials.

References

Alexander RE. 1974. *Applications of Bioassay of Uranium*. WASH 1251, U.S. Nuclear Regulatory Commission, Washington, DC.

ANSI N317-1980 (Reaffirmed 1991). *Performance Criteria for Instrumentation Used for Inplant Plutonium Monitoring*. American National Standards Institute, NY.

Ballinger MY and RB Hall. 1991. *A History of Major Hanford Facilities and Processes Involving Radioactive Material*. PNL-6964 HEDR, Pacific Northwest Laboratory, Richland, WA.

Rokkan DJ, K Rhoads, and LH Staven. 2002. *Calculating Potential-to-Emit Releases and Doses for FEMPs and NOCs*. HNF-3602, Revision 1, Fluor Hanford, Richland, WA.

Shleien B, LA Slaback Jr, and BK Birky. 1998. *Handbook of Health Physics and Radiological Health*, Third Edition, Lippincott Williams & Wilkins, New York, NY.

Sula MJ, EH Carbaugh, and DE Bihl. 1991. *Technical Basis for Internal Dosimetry at Hanford*. PNL-6866, Rev 1, Pacific Northwest Laboratory, Richland, WA.

Appendix C

Comparison of EPA with PNNL Radiological Air Task Documents

Appendix C

Comparison of EPA *Recommendations for a Uniform Protocol for Periodic Confirmatory Measurements of "Minor" Air Emissions Sources Subject to 40 CFR Part 61, Subpart H* (May 9, 2007) with PNNL Radiological Air Task Documents

Recommendations for Periodic Confirmatory Measurements (PCMs)	• **PNNL-10855, Rev. 5,** *Assessment of Unabated Facility Emission Potentials for Evaluating Airborne Radionuclide Monitoring Requirements at Pacific Northwest National Laboratory – 2010* • **PNNL Potential Impact Categories, October 2010, Rev. 3** • **EM-QA-01, Rev. 7,** *Effluent Management Quality Assurance Plan* • **PNNL-15992,** *300 Area Pacific Northwest National Laboratory Facility Radionuclide Emission Points and Sampling Systems (Barfuss, Barnett, and Ballinger 2009)*
(1) GRADED APPROACH TO CLASSIFICATION SYSTEM: Describe how minor sources are subdivided and the basis for each classification.	The PNNL potential impact categories (PICs) document specifies the basis for minor source categories and identifies a PIC for each PNNL minor source.
(2) METHODS FOR PCM: Methods used to confirm that minor sources are correctly categorized (e.g., emissions measurement, radionuclide inventory).	PNNL-10855 describes the methodology for completing the annual NESHAP assessment. The annual assessments use current radionuclide inventory for each building.
(3) SUPPORTIVE DATA: • Meteorological • Release Fractions • Materials volatilization temperatures • MEI selection method	• The Hanford Meteorological Station provides meteorological measurements. Dose modeling meteorological data are published in the appendix of the annual air emission report for the Hanford Site (i.e., DOE/RL-2010-17). • Release fractions described in PNNL-10855. • Materials volatilization temperatures considered in potential release-fraction determinations, PNNL-10855 • MEI selection for the Hanford Site emissions described in the *Calculating Potential-to-Emit Radiological Release and Doses* (DOE/RL-2006-29). • MEI selection for the PNNL Site emissions described in *PNNL Site Dose-per-Unit-Release Factors for Using Calculating Radionuclide Air Emissions Potential-to-Emit Doses* (PNNL-17847).
(4) DISPERSION/DOSE MODEL USED: The reason for using any code other than CAP-88 version 3 should be explained.	CAP88-PC used for dispersion modeling as described in PNNL-10855.°
(5) QUALITY CONTROL ASPECTS: Quality assurance activities performed on a minor source should be consistent with a graded approach.	EM-QA-01 details quality assurance methods in place to validate the data gathering and reporting process. Standard operating procedures are implemented for related work (e.g., sampling activities) and updated biennially.
(6) FREQUENCY OF CONFIRMATION: The frequency that source emissions will be confirmed by sampling or other means.	PNNL-10855 describes the annual NESHAP assessment methodology. The Washington Department of Health permits specify monitoring requirements and sampling frequencies. Current sampling frequencies are maintained in the Gaseous Effluent Database and documented in PNNL-15992. Note: Although the TE) for each emission unit is calculated annually using actual radionuclide inventory, the PTE used for assigning PICs should be the permitted PTE, which is based on maximum estimated inventory and throughput for permitted activities.

° As noted in this document, unit doses for the 300 Area are planned to be updated to DOE/RL-2006-29, Revision 1 by January 2011 and the LMFs for the Richland facilities will be updated at the same time. The revision is based on CAP-88 version 3.

Distribution

No. of
Copies

2 **Washington Department of Health**

    JW Schmidt   B1-42
    RJ Utley   B1-42

1 **U.S. Department of Energy, Pacific Northwest Site Office**

    TL Aldridge   K9-42

1 **U.S. Department of Energy, Richland Operations Office**

    DE Jackson   A4-52

13 **Pacific Northwest National Laboratory**

    MY Ballinger   BSRC
    JM Barnett (3)   J2-25
    EG Damberg   J2-25
    PM Daling   J2-50
    TL Gervais   J2-25
    RD Sharp   J4-50
    MJ Stephenson   J2-25
    EM File Plan T07.3.1.1.1 J2-25
    HTL (2)   P8-55

Pacific Northwest
NATIONAL LABORATORY

Proudly Operated by **Battelle** *Since 1965*

U.S. DEPARTMENT OF
ENERGY

902 Battelle Boulevard
P.O. Box 999
Richland, WA 99352
1-888-375-PNNL (7665)
www.pnl.gov